I MOVED ON, NOW WHAT?

Poems And Writing Prompts
for Healing
A Broken Heart.

By Tony Sanwo

ISBN: 9798386844561

Contents

Intro

Love can bring us great joy and comfort, but also great pain. When a relationship comes to an end, the loss can feel devastating, as if a piece of our heart has been ripped away. We may feel lost, alone, and uncertain of what the future holds. But even amid heartbreak, there is hope.

This collection of poems is inspired by the experience of love coming to an end. The pain and sadness that follows are always intense and it takes time to heal. Through self-reflection and personal growth, you can find a way to move forward and find new meaning in life.

There is the pain of loss and grief, the confusion of unanswered questions, and the anger and bitterness that can arise after a breakup. But there is also reflection, acceptance, and the promise of growth and renewal.

Here is an opportunity to heal through words and your writing. With the deep emotions felt through a breakup, there needs to be an outlet to express one's pain and disbelief.

Following the poems in this collection is a series of guided writing prompts that will help you come to terms with the relationship you once had and allow you to rediscover yourself so you can really move on.

If you are currently going through a breakup or simply looking for solace and hope amid difficult times, this book offers a powerful avenue for recovery. The main message is that even when love ends and life goes on, we need to go through healing to start anew.

The Breakup

Brokenhearted

I never thought it would end this way,
Our love was strong, or so I thought,
But now I sit here, brokenhearted,
Wondering how it all fell apart.

I thought we had forever,
But forever turned out to be just a moment,
And now I'm left with nothing,
But memories of what we once had.

My heart is heavy with sorrow,
As I try to make sense of it all,
How did we go from love to strangers,
So quickly, so suddenly, so wrong?

I remember the days we laughed,
And the nights we held each other tight,
But now those moments are gone,
Leaving me alone in the dark of night.

I try to pick up the pieces,
But they slip through my fingers like sand,
Leaving me lost and brokenhearted,
Wondering how I'll ever love again.

But I know that I must move on,

And though the road ahead is steep,
I will find my way through the darkness,
And emerge into the light of day.

For though my heart is broken,
I know that it will heal in time,
And I'll look back on this moment,
As just another step on the journey of life.

The Day You Left

The day you left, my world fell apart,
And nothing felt the same,
I felt like I was lost at sea,
Without a guiding flame.

The sun was shining bright that day,
But all I felt was rain,
My heart was heavy with sadness,
As I tried to ease the pain.

I remember the way you looked at me,
With eyes so warm and true,
But now those eyes are gone,
Leaving me feeling so blue.

I try to fill the emptiness,
With memories of what we had,
But they only make me miss you more,
And feel so very sad.

I wish that I could turn back time,
And make things right again,
But I know that's just a dream,
A fantasy that's at an end.

The day you left, a part of me,

Went with you on your way,
Leaving me to pick up the pieces,
Of a love that couldn't stay.

But I will find my way again,
And though the road is long,
I'll learn to live without you,
And find a new place to belong.

For though the day you left was hard,
And left my heart in pain,
I know that I will survive,
And learn to love again.

Shattered Dreams

My heart was full of hope and love,
As we started down the path,
But somewhere along the way,
Our love began to crack.

We had such big dreams,
Of a future bright and true,
But now those dreams are shattered,
Leaving me feeling so blue.

I thought we'd be forever,
But forever turned out to be,
Just a fleeting moment in time,
A mere memory of what could be.

The love we shared was special,
And I'll always cherish it so,
But now I'm left with nothing,
But a heart that's filled with woe.

I try to piece together,
What went wrong and where we strayed,
But the answers elude me,
Like a mirage in the desert shade.

I wish that we could start anew,

And try again to find,
The love that once we shared,
And heal the wounds of time.

But I know that's just a fantasy,
A dream that cannot be,
For the shattered pieces of our love,
Are too many to retrieve.

I'll move on, brokenhearted,
And try to find my way,
Through the darkness of this moment,
And into a brighter day.

My dreams are shattered,
And my heart is full of pain,
I know that I'll survive this,
And find love once again.

Painful Goodbyes

It hurts to say goodbye,
To the one who held my heart,
To the one who made me laugh,
And helped me heal my scars.

It hurts to watch you go,
To see you walk away,
To know that what we had,
Is gone without a trace.

The memories flood my mind,
Of all the good times shared,
Of the laughter and the love,
That once we freely bared.

But now those days are gone,
And all that's left is pain,
The hurt of what we lost,
And the tears that fall like rain.

It's hard to say goodbye,
To the one you thought was true,
To the one who was your everything,
But now that love is through.

I know that time will heal,

The wounds that now we bear,
But in this moment of goodbye,
All I feel is despair.

I wish that we could turn back time,
And start our love anew,
But I know that's just a fantasy,
And there's nothing left to do.

I'll say goodbye with grace,
And try to move on strong,
For in the pain of goodbye,
I'll find a love that will belong.

I know this love is over,
And my heart is full of pain,
I know that in the future,
A love that's true will reign.

Lost and Alone

In the darkness of my room,
I sit here all alone,
Lost in the memories,
Of a love that's gone and flown.

The silence is suffocating,
As I try to catch my breath,
My heart is shattered into pieces,
And my soul is lost in death.

The emptiness surrounds me,
As I reach out for your touch,
But all that's left is emptiness,
And the pain is just too much.

I thought that we were forever,
That our love would never fade,
But now I'm lost and alone,
And the memories are all that's stayed.

The nights are filled with tears,
As I lay here in my bed,
Thinking of what could have been,
And the love that's now just dead.

I try to fill the void,

With the memories that we shared,
But all I feel is emptiness,
And the pain is just too hard to bear.

The love we had is gone,
And I'm left here all alone,
Lost in the memories,
Of a love that's never coming home.

But though the pain is deep,
And the tears just won't subside,
I know that I'll get through this,
And find a love that's right.

The Aftermath

In the aftermath of our love,
I'm left here all alone,
Lost in the memories of what we had,
And the pain that's now been shown.

The days are long and lonely,
As I try to move ahead,
But the love we shared is gone,
And my heart is filled with dread.

The silence is suffocating,
As I search for what went wrong,
But all that's left is emptiness,
And the memories that belong.

The laughter and the joy we shared,
Are now just faded dreams,
And though I try to move ahead,
The pain just won't redeem.

The future once so bright and clear,
Is now shrouded in doubt and fear,
As I try to pick up the pieces,
Of a love that's no longer here.

Though the pain is deep,

And the tears just won't subside,
I know that I'll get through this,
And find a love that's right.

Though our love is gone,
And the memories are all that's left,
I'll move ahead and find a way,
To heal and find new strength.

Bitter Regrets

In the stillness of the night,
When the memories come to call,
I'm haunted by the bitter regrets,
Of a love that had to fall.

The words we spoke, the tears we shed,
Are now just echoes in my head,
And though I try to forget it all,
The pain just won't subside at all.

I wish that I could turn back time,
And mend the wounds that we both made,
But now it's all too late to try,
And the price of love has been paid.

The regrets are like a poison,
That fills my heart with pain,
As I look back on what we had,
And the love that we couldn't sustain.

Though the regrets may linger,
And the pain may never fade,
I know that I'll find a way to heal,
And find love again someday.

Though our love may be gone,

And the regrets are all that's left,
I'll find the strength to move ahead,
And leave behind this bitter theft.

Here's to the love that we once had,
And the memories that we shared,
May we find the peace we need,
And the strength to keep on, unimpaired.

Memories Haunt Me

The memories of you still linger,
Haunting me like a ghost,
The love we shared, the dreams we had,
All gone, like a forgotten host.

I try to move on, to forget,
But your memory lingers on,
The times we laughed, the times we wept,
The memories of you, they won't be gone.

The moments we shared, the love we made,
All a distant dream now,
The pain of losing you, it won't fade,
The hurt, it's always somehow.

I thought we had a future,
That our love was meant to be,
But now I'm left with memories,
Of a love that wasn't meant to be.

The nights are the hardest,
When I'm left alone with my thoughts,
The memories, they come flooding back,
And my heart, it feels so fraught.

But even though the pain remains,

And the memories, they won't let go,
I know that I'll find a way to heal,
And let your memory finally go.

Though the memories may haunt me,
And the pain may never fade,
I'll find the strength to move ahead,
And leave behind this love that's frayed.

Torn Apart

We were once two halves of a whole,
Our love was strong, unbreakable,
But now we're torn apart,
And the pain, it's unmistakable.

Our love was like a fire,
Burning bright and true,
But now the flames have died down,
And I'm left feeling so blue.

The memories of you still linger,
Haunting me like a ghost,
The love we shared, the dreams we had,
All gone, like a forgotten host.

I thought we'd last forever,
That our love was built to last,
But now we're just two strangers,
With a love that's in the past.

The pain of losing you, it's real,
It's like a knife that cuts so deep,
And even though I know I should move on,
My heart just can't seem to keep.

But even though we're torn apart,

And our love has come to an end,
I know that I'll find a way to heal,
And my heart, it will mend.

Though the pain may linger,
And the memories, they won't depart,
I'll find the strength to move ahead,
And heal this broken heart.

Unanswered Questions

In the silence of my thoughts,
The memories come flooding back,
Of a love that once was strong,
But now it's all turned black.

So many unanswered questions,
Lingering in my mind,
Why did our love have to end,
And leave us both behind?

Was it something I said,
Or something I didn't do?
Did I take our love for granted,
And not cherish it like I should?

Or was it you, my love,
Who let our love slip away,
Did you grow tired of me,
And decide you couldn't stay?

I'm left with all these questions,
And the answers, they elude,
Leaving me lost and confused,
And feeling so subdued.

But even in the midst of the pain,

I know that life goes on,
And though our love may be broken,
My spirit, it will stay strong.

I'll keep searching for the answers,
And the truth, it will be revealed,
And maybe, just maybe,
My broken heart, it will be healed.

Self-Reflection

Rebuilding Myself

I stand before the mirror,
Staring at my reflection.
The person I once knew,
Is a mere recollection.

The breakup shattered me,
Left me in pieces on the floor.
But as the dust settles,
I begin to rebuild once more.

I start with self-love,
Treating myself with care.
Finding worth in myself,
Not searching for it out there.

I delve into my passions,
Rediscovering old and new.
Finding joy in the simple things,
That once seemed so few.

I confront my fears,
No longer running away.
Facing them head-on,
To live another day.

I discover my strength,

And the resilience within.
Realizing I can survive,
No matter what life may bring.

The scars may remain,
But they tell a story of growth.
Of a person who rebuilt,
From the ashes of a breakup's oath.

Now I stand before the mirror,
A new reflection in my eyes.
One that glimmers with hope,
And a heart that's learned to rise.

I am rebuilding myself,
Not just fixing the broken parts.
But creating something new,
From the depths of my heart.

The Journey Within

I took a journey deep inside
To find the person I hide
Behind the walls I built up high
To keep me safe, to shield my cry.

I searched through memories of old.
Of love and loss, of stories untold
And found the pieces of my heart.
That were broken and torn apart.

But in the darkness, there was light.
A flicker of hope, a shining bright
I saw myself in a different way.
Not broken, not lost, but strong and brave.

I embraced the pain and the hurt.
And learned to love all that I am worth.
I let go of the past and the pain.
And found a new purpose, a new gain.

In the journey within
I found the strength to begin
A new chapter, a new story
Full of hope, full of glory

I am not the same as before

But stronger, wiser, and so much more
In the journey within
I found myself, and a new beginning.

Discovering My Strengths

Amidst the turmoil of heartbreak and pain,
I sought to find myself once again.
To rediscover who I truly am,
And find the strength to carry on and stand.

I searched within, with a soulful gaze,
Uncovering truths that had been in a haze.
I realized the beauty of my flaws,
And the strength that lay within my scars.

I found a newfound confidence and grace,
As I learned to embrace my unique face.
I discovered passions that set my heart ablaze,
And dreams that fueled me for endless days.

I learned to love myself, flaws and all,
And stood tall, proud and strong, feeling ten feet tall.
No longer held back by fear or doubt,
I embarked on a journey to a life without.

Now, with a renewed sense of self,
I walk the path that is meant for myself.
Empowered by the strength I've discovered,
I know I can conquer any obstacle uncovered.

Unearthing Hidden Passions

In the depths of heartache and despair
I found a spark, a flame, a glare.
A passion that was buried deep.
A dream I thought I couldn't keep.

With every shattered piece of my heart
A new passion was ready to start.
I dug and searched within my soul.
To find the parts that made me whole.

I explored my thoughts and deepest fears.
And let go of my past and tears.
I rediscovered what made me me
And found a passion I never thought I'd see.

The world was wide and full of light.
As I discovered a new sight
I was not limited by the past.
And found a new joy that would forever last.

I followed my heart and let it lead.
To new passions that I did not heed
I found the courage to take a chance.
And discovered a new life, a new dance.

If you feel lost and without direction

Take a deep breath and find connection.
Within yourself there's a treasure trove
Of passions waiting to be unearthed and loved.

Embracing My Flaws

I stand before the mirror,
Gazing at my reflection,
My flaws and imperfections,
Are etched upon my complexion.

For years I've been ashamed,
Of the scars and marks I bear,
But now I see their beauty,
And the stories they have to share.

I am not perfect,
But that's okay with me,
For I am flawed and human,
And that's who I am meant to be.

I used to hide behind masks,
Afraid to let others see,
But now I embrace my flaws,
And set my true self free.

No longer do I compare,
Myself to someone else,
For I am unique and special,
And that's something to be proud of.

My flaws are my strengths,

And my scars are my badge,
Of all that I have overcome,
And the battles that I've waged.

I embrace my imperfections,
And hold my head up high,
For I am beautifully flawed,
And that's the reason why.

Falling in Love with Myself

I used to think love was something outside of me,
A prize to be won, a person to see.
I searched high and low, left and right,
For someone to complete me, to hold me tight.

But as the years went by and the loves came and went,
I realized that my heart was still deeply bent.
Bent on finding love outside of myself,
Blind to the love I needed from no one else.

It took some time and a lot of tears,
To see that the love I sought was already near.
It was in the way I laughed and the way I cried,
In the way I danced and the way I sighed.

I began to see my flaws as beautiful things,
And love myself despite my stumbles and wings.
I learned to be gentle and kind with my soul,
And embrace the parts of me that make me whole.

I fell in love with my curves and my edges,
The way my eyes light up when I smile at my reflections.
I embraced the power that was always within,
And let go of the notion that love was outside of my skin.

Now I love myself fiercely, with all my heart,

And I know that I never have to be apart
From the love that I seek, the love that I need,
For it's been inside me all along, indeed.

The Power of Self-Care

I used to think love was all I needed,
A love that was strong, passionate and heated.
But I soon discovered, it wasn't quite so,
For when that love was gone, I felt so low.

I tried to fill the void with someone new,
But it was never the same, it never quite grew.
So I turned inward, to the depths of my soul,
To discover what makes me feel whole.

I started with self-care, a small act of love,
Taking care of myself, like a precious dove.
A bubble bath here, a walk in the sun,
Taking time to relax, to just have fun.

I realized how little I knew of myself,
So I explored my interests, my passions, my wealth.
I started writing, painting, and dancing too,
I found new talents I never knew.

I embraced my flaws, my imperfections,
I learned to love myself without exceptions.
I found my strength, my power within,
And soon the journey became a win.

I fell in love with myself, in every way,

And it changed my life, day by day.
The power of self-care, I cannot ignore,
It opened up new doors, and so much more.

If you're feeling lost, or feeling low,
Turn to self-care, and let it grow.
Discover the beauty, the power within,
And soon your life will begin to spin.

Redefining Happiness

I used to think that love was all I needed,
That without it, my life would never be completed.
But now I know that love is not enough,
That true happiness comes from within, it's a rebuff.

I've learned that I am enough, just as I am,
And I don't need someone else to be my biggest fan.
I'm learning to love myself, flaws and all,
And finding happiness in things both big and small.

I'm rediscovering passions I had set aside,
And finding joy in the things that make me feel alive.
I'm taking time for self-care, both mind and soul,
And finding peace in the things that make me whole.

I'm embracing the journey of self-discovery,
And realizing that true happiness is a possibility.
It's not about finding someone else to complete me,
It's about falling in love with myself, finally feeling free.

Here's to redefining what happiness means,
To finding joy in the present and in future dreams.
To realizing that I am enough, just as I am,
And living a life full of love, happiness, and self-reflection.

Finding Peace Within

In the depths of my soul, I search for peace,
For solace from the pain that will not cease.
Through winding paths of self-reflection,
I journey on towards introspection.

I face my fears, my doubts, my flaws,
And learn to love myself without pause.
For in the moments of pure self-care,
I find the strength to repair.

The scars of heartbreak slowly fade,
As I embrace the beauty in the shade.
For darkness need not mean despair,
But rather a chance for hope to repair.

I find new passions deep within,
And breathe in the air of change again.
For life is too short to stay confined,
To walls of hurt that seem to bind.

I redefine what happiness means,
And let go of what no longer brings me dreams.
For the love I seek is first within,
And only then can I let love in.

And as I journey through this life,

I find the peace that heals my strife.
For in the depths of my own soul,
I find the strength to be whole.

The Beauty of Self-Discovery

Through the journey of life,
There are moments of strife,
Where we question our place,
And the choices we embrace.

We wonder who we are,
And if we've come this far,
With purpose and intent,
Or by sheer accident.

But in the depths of our soul,
Lies the power to unfold,
The secrets that we keep,
And the truths that we seek.

For it's in self-discovery,
That we find our destiny,
And the beauty of our being,
Is revealed in our seeing.

The world becomes a canvas,
And our lives a work of art,
As we paint the colors of our essence,
With every beat of our heart.

We embrace our strengths and flaws,

And find joy in the simple cause,
Of being true to ourselves,
And letting go of all else.

For in the beauty of self-discovery,
We find the path to true recovery,
And the light that guides us through,
Is the love we have for me and you.

Healing and Moving On

Wounds that Heal

I once thought my heart was shattered
Beyond repair, my soul battered
But time, like a gentle balm,
Has soothed the wounds, brought calm.

Each day, I take one step forward,
Away from pain, towards a new world.
I no longer hold onto grudges or hate,
For it is forgiveness that seals my fate.

I have learned to embrace my flaws,
And to never let anyone else's opinion cause
Me to doubt my worth or my beauty,
For I am unique and deserving of love and duty.

The scars on my heart are reminders
Of the journey I've taken, the battles fought.
But they no longer define me or hinder
The person I am, the life I've sought.

I am stronger for what I've been through,
Resilient, determined, and true.
I am grateful for the wounds that heal,
For they have shown me what is real.

Love can be fleeting, but self-love is eternal,

And it is this love that has made me internal.
The beauty of life, the power of hope,
And the strength to heal, to cope.

Let the wounds heal, let the heart mend,
For in the end, it is our spirit that ascends.
We rise above the pain and the hurt,
And find the beauty in our worth.

A New Dawn

A new dawn has come, and I am reborn,
No longer weighed down by the past forlorn.
I've shed the tears, and faced the pain,
And in its place, found strength to gain.

The wounds may have been deep,
But they did not break me, nor my spirit steep.
For in each trial, there was a lesson to learn,
And in each heartbreak, a new page to turn.

I've learned to forgive, both myself and the other,
To let go of the anger, and find peace in the smother.
The bitterness no longer lingers,
As I release the pain with my fingers.

And with each breath, a new life blooms,
As I shed the weight of old wounds.
A new chapter begins, full of hope and light,
As I take on the world with all my might.

For I am not broken, nor am I weak,
But a warrior who has found the strength to seek,
A new dawn, a new life, a new me,
Full of love, joy, and all that could be.

Closure

In search of peace, I longed for closure
To bid farewell, to end the exposure
Of heartbreak, pain, and endless tears
And move on from my darkest fears

But closure, oh how it seemed so far
A wound that refused to heal, a scar
That reminded me of the past so clear
A weight too heavy for me to bear

I sought for answers, for a reason why
A need to know, to finally comply
With the end of an era, a love that died
To finally let go and turn the tide

And so I searched within my soul
To find the strength to reach my goal
To forgive, to accept, to finally see
That closure lies within me

I let go of resentment and anger
And found comfort in forgiveness, a new anchor
I faced my fears and embraced my pain
And found beauty in the scars that remain

For they are reminders of my strength

Of how I survived, and endured the length
Of a love that once was, but now is gone
A new beginning, a brand new dawn

I bid farewell, to the past that was
And embrace the future, with open arms
For closure lies within, it's always been
A journey of healing, a path to win.

Breaking the Chains

I used to feel so trapped
Held down by your chains
I thought I was nothing without you
But I was wrong, I had to change

I had to break the chains
That kept me locked in your hold
I had to find the strength
To break free and be bold

It wasn't easy, I'll admit
There were moments of doubt and pain
But I knew I couldn't stay
In a love that was only feign

I stood up and walked away
Leaving you and our past behind
And though it hurt to say goodbye
I knew it was time to find

A life that was truly mine
One where I could soar and fly
Where I could discover my worth
And finally learn to thrive

It's been a journey, I won't lie

But I've found joy in every step
I've learned to love myself again
And to never ever forget

That I am strong and I am free
And my life is my own to lead
I've broken the chains that held me down
And now I am finally free.

Forgiveness

In the depths of my soul, I carry a weight
A burden of hurt and anger that I can't escape
I've been wronged and hurt, betrayed and mistreated
And the thought of forgiveness, at first, seemed conceited

But as time passed by, and wounds started to heal
I realized that holding onto the pain was not ideal
It weighed me down, kept me from moving on
And the only way to break free was to forgive and be strong

It's not an easy path, forgiving those who caused harm
But it's necessary for my own healing and calm
To release the bitterness, the grudges, and the hate
And instead, let love and compassion take their place

Forgiveness is not forgetting, it's not excusing the wrong
It's about letting go of the hurt and moving on
It's a choice, a conscious decision to set myself free
And embrace the peace and joy that come with inner harmony

I choose to forgive, to let go of the past
To move forward with grace, love, and steadfast
I release the chains of anger, bitterness, and blame
And in their place, I welcome freedom, love, and a new flame

Forgiveness is not weakness, it's an act of strength

It's a way to break the cycle of hurt and pain
And with each step forward, each act of forgiveness
I'm reclaiming my power, and healing my own brokenness.

The Power of Letting Go

The power of letting go,
Is a skill we all must know,
To release the hurt and pain,
And start living once again.

It's not an easy feat,
To surrender and retreat,
From the love we held so tight,
And now must release in flight.

But in letting go we find,
A freedom of the mind,
A chance to start anew,
And begin life with a view.

Of all the possibilities,
And endless opportunities,
To explore and to grow,
And let our true selves show.

We learn to forgive and forget,
And move on without regret,
To love ourselves and others,
And embrace life like no other.

For letting go is not a loss,

But a gain at any cost,
A gift we give to ourselves,
To heal and love like never else.

Let us all learn to release,
And find inner peace,
In the power of letting go,
And the happiness that will flow.

Rebuilding from the Ashes

From the ashes of my pain and sorrow,
I rise up, renewed, and full of power.
For though I may have been broken down,
I refuse to be defeated, or to drown.

I gather up the pieces of my shattered heart,
And piece them back together, part by part.
With every stitch, I feel myself grow strong,
And though the process may be long,
I know that I will come out whole,
With scars that tell a story of my soul.

I find strength in the depths of my despair,
And with every breath, I clear the air
Of all the toxic thoughts and fears,
That kept me captive all these years.

I break the chains that held me back,
And move forward, unburdened and intact.
I let go of all the pain and strife,
And embrace a new and better life.

For I know that I am more than what was lost,
And in this journey, I have paid the cost.
But with every step, I gain more ground,
And in my heart, a new hope is found.

Let the fires rage and burn,
For from the ashes, I will return.
Stronger, braver, and more alive,
Ready to take on whatever life may thrive.

For I am a phoenix, rising from the flame,
Reborn anew, and unafraid to claim
My place in this world, and to stand tall,
For I have risen from the ashes, and conquered all.

From Pain to Strength

From pain to strength, I rise again,
My heart once shattered, now on the mend,
I've felt the depths of sorrow and woe,
But now I'm standing tall, with a newfound glow.

In the midst of darkness, I found a light,
A flicker of hope that burned so bright,
I clung to it with all my might,
And it carried me through the longest night.

I've shed my tears and cried my pain,
But I've emerged stronger, no longer in vain,
For the pain that once held me down,
Has now become the strength that helps me rebound.

I've learned to let go of what's not meant to be,
And to hold on to the blessings that set me free,
I've found the power to forgive and move on,
And to see the beauty in what once seemed gone.

I've embraced the scars that tell my story,
And wear them proudly, no longer in worry,
For they remind me of my journey so far,
And the strength I've gained from every scar.

Let the pain be a reminder of what I've overcome,

And let my strength be a beacon to all who've succumbed,
In the midst of darkness, there is always a light,
And in the face of adversity, there is always a fight.

From pain to strength, I rise again,
My heart once shattered, now on the mend,
For I am a survivor, a warrior, a force to be reckoned,
And with every step, I am closer to my redemption.

The Art of Moving On

In the depths of pain and sorrow,
When all hope seems to fade away,
It's hard to imagine a tomorrow,
When the heart is heavy and grey.

But as time passes and wounds begin to heal,
The heart slowly starts to mend,
And though it may seem surreal,
The broken pieces begin to blend.

It's a process that can't be rushed,
For true healing takes its time,
And though the journey may be hushed,
It's a journey towards the sublime.

The art of moving on is an intricate dance,
Of letting go and embracing the new,
Of learning from past mistakes and taking a chance,
On a future that's fresh and true.

It's not about forgetting or pretending it's all okay,
But rather about accepting what cannot be changed,
And finding a way to pave a new way,
One that's brighter and rearranged.

It's about releasing the pain and the hurt,

And choosing to focus on the good,
For only then can true joy and peace assert,
And the future be fully understood.

Let go of what no longer serves,
And embrace what's yet to come,
For the art of moving on deserves,
A heart that's open and some.

May we all find the strength to let go,
And embrace the beauty that life holds,
For in doing so, we can truly grow,
And the story of our lives will unfold.

Resilience

Resilience, the strength within,
To rise again, to start again,
A will to live, to breathe, to win,
A faith in oneself, to ease the pain.

It's the art of bouncing back,
Of standing tall, after a fall,
A heart that mends the crack,
A spirit that answers the call.

It's the power of a flower,
That blooms in the darkest hour,
A light that shines with might,
A vision that never loses sight.

Resilience is the shield,
That guards us in life's battlefield,
A force that empowers,
A flame that never cowers.

It's the courage to face the storm,
To weather it and transform,
To embrace life's change,
And find beauty in the strange.

Resilience is the lesson learned,

From the scars that never burned,
From the tears that never drowned,
From the dreams that never found.

It's the journey to healing,
To find the peace that's revealing,
To cherish every moment,
And live life to the fullest extent.

Resilience is the treasure,
That lies within us, with pleasure,
To know that we can overcome,
And rise again, with the strength of a thousand suns.

Let us embrace our resilience,
With grace, and love, and persistence,
For it is the gift we own,
To thrive, to heal, to be reborn.

Looking to the Future

Rising from the Ashes

Out of the rubble and debris,
I rise from the ashes of my past,
With a newfound strength and resilience,
To face the future with hope at last.

The flames of heartbreak and loss,
Once consumed my very soul,
But now I see a path before me,
And I know I can take control.

I am not defined by my failures,
Nor am I held back by my fears,
For I have learned to embrace the unknown,
And to welcome the promise of new years.

Though the scars of the past may linger,
I am not bound to their grip,
For I am a warrior of my own making,
And I will not let my spirit slip.

Let the winds of change carry me,
To lands beyond my wildest dreams,
For I am a phoenix rising,
From the ashes of what once seemed.

And with each step I take forward,

I am reminded of my worth,
For I am a survivor and a fighter,
And my future is what I unearth.

The Promise of a New Day

I wake to the promise of a new day,
With renewed hope and a spirit that's gay.
Yesterday's sorrows are now put aside,
As I focus on the future, with a heart open wide.

The sun's warm rays greet me with a smile,
As I embrace the day with a sense of style.
A new beginning, a fresh start,
I feel the beating of my rejuvenated heart.

I leave behind the memories that caused me pain,
And embrace the future, with its vast terrain.
The possibilities are endless, the horizon bright,
I spread my wings, take off in flight.

With every step I take, I feel more free,
My spirit soaring, filled with glee.
I am not alone, for the universe is my guide,
Leading me to a future where I'll thrive.

I am ready to face whatever comes my way,
For I know I am strong enough to seize the day.
I'll take the lessons learned from yesterday,
And use them to pave the path to a brighter way.

Now I walk with my head held high,

Filled with a new sense of purpose and drive.
The promise of a new day is here to stay,
And I am ready to embrace it in every way.

A Road to Redemption

Onward and upward, my journey begins,
A new chapter of life, I'm ready to win.
I've been through the fire, I've been through the rain,
But I'm still standing, and I feel no pain.

The road ahead is long and winding,
But I'm determined, and I'll keep climbing.
I'll shed the old me, and embrace the new,
I'll leave the past behind, and start anew.

The wounds may still be fresh, the hurt may still remain,
But I'll find the strength to rise again.
I'll learn from my mistakes, I'll grow from the pain,
I'll turn my heartache into gain.

With each step I take, I'll leave the past behind,
I'll heal my broken heart, and free my troubled mind.
I'll find my way back to love, and trust again,
And start a new chapter with a better end.

The journey may be tough, but I'll be tougher,
I'll rise above it all, and I'll be a conqueror.
I'll stand tall, and I'll stand strong,
And I'll keep moving forward, where I belong.

Here's to the future, and all it holds in store,

I'm ready to embrace it, and I'll do so much more.

I'll build a new life, and I'll make it great,

And the road to redemption, will have been worth the wait.

The Renewal of Self

In the aftermath of love lost,
I found myself adrift at sea,
A shell of who I used to be,
But within the wreckage, at what cost?

I discovered something new,
The power of self-renewal,
The ability to mend what's residual,
To embrace the changes, and start anew.

I found consolation in my solitude,
And found the strength to carry on,
To seek out a brighter dawn,
To let go of the pain and conclude.

The renewal of self is a journey,
One that takes patience and grace,
But within the struggle, we can find space,
To emerge stronger, and live freely.

For in the midst of our darkest hour,
We can find a glimmer of hope,
A way to break free from the ropes,
And rise above the world's overpower.

So let us embrace the renewal of self,

And find the courage to move forward,
To leave behind the past's discord,
And focus on what's to come, a new self.

Breaking Free

I've shed the skin of my past self,
Embraced the future, and my new wealth.
My heart, once broken, now beats anew,
A rhythm of hope and dreams anew.

I'm breaking free from the chains that bind,
The memories that weigh heavy on my mind.
I'm standing tall, my head held high,
A new beginning, a fresh start, I'll never again lie.

I've walked through fire and emerged unscathed,
My strength and courage once again displayed.
I've learned to let go of what's not meant to be,
And embrace the beauty in what's yet to come, to see.

I'm breaking free from the fear that held me back,
The doubt and insecurity, I'm on the right track.
The journey ahead may be filled with strife,
But I know that I'm ready to tackle life.

The past is gone, it's time to move on,
To embrace the present, and what's yet to come.
I'm breaking free, spreading my wings,
Soaring towards my dreams, and all the wonderful things.

I've learned to love myself, flaws and all,

And to embrace the beauty of standing tall.
I'm breaking free from what once held me down,
And rising up, a queen with a crown.

The future's bright, and full of endless possibility,
A world of wonder and love, a life of tranquility.
I'm breaking free, embracing the unknown,
And stepping forward into the light, into the new dawn.

The Art of Letting Go

The art of letting go is not easy to master,
It takes strength and courage to break away from disaster.
To release what once was and move on to what can be,
Is a journey of growth, a process of setting oneself free.

Letting go is like shedding old skin,
A necessary step for new beginnings to begin.
It can be painful, it can be tough,
But it's necessary to make way for new love.

We hold on to memories that are too dear,
And it becomes a burden that we can't bear.
But the weight of the past can be lifted,
If we choose to let go and accept what is gifted.

It's the art of letting go that opens new doors,
A path to peace, a chance to explore.
It's the key to unlock our hearts,
And start fresh, making a brand new start.

The art of letting go is an act of grace,
To honor the past and embrace a new space.
It's a powerful act of self-love,
A new chapter in the story of us.

So let go of the pain and embrace the light,

Trust in the journey, trust in what's right.
For the art of letting go is the way to heal,
And it's the first step towards a life that's real.

A Journey to Self-Discovery

I walk along the path of life,
With the shadows of my past behind
The weight of my mistakes and strife
Bearing heavy on my mind.

But as I journey on, I see
A light that shines ahead of me
The promise of a new tomorrow
Where I can leave my pain and sorrow.

I take a step, and then another
Leaving behind my fears and troubles
For every step is like no other
A chance to break free from my struggles.

I am on a journey of self-discovery
To find the person I was meant to be
To shed the old and embrace the new
To live a life that is pure and true.

I seek the wisdom of the ages
To help me find my inner truth
To write my story on life's pages
With each chapter full of hope and youth.

The road is long and winding

But I am strong and resolute
For every step, I am finding
A new sense of purpose and pursuit.

With each dawn, I am reborn
Ready to face what lies ahead
My past may be tattered and torn
But my future is mine to be led.

So, I continue on this path
With a heart full of hope and faith
For I know that every trial and wrath
Will lead me to my destined fate.

A journey to self-discovery
Is not for the faint of heart
But for those who seek to be free
It is the only way to start.

For in the end, I will emerge
A new creation, whole and pure
My soul unburdened, free to surge
Towards the future, strong and sure.

I am on a journey of self-discovery
A road to freedom, a path to me
With each step, I am growing
Into the person I was meant to be.

The Light Ahead

I've weathered many storms,
And braved the darkest of nights.
I've wandered through the wilderness,
And fought with all my might.

But even in the toughest times,
When I could barely see,
A tiny light was shining,
And it was calling out to me.

I stumbled and I fell,
And often lost my way,
But that light kept burning brighter,
As I faced each new day.

It was the promise of tomorrow,
The hope that I could be,
Something more than I was yesterday,
Something stronger, wild and free.

I walked towards that light,
With every step I took,
The past was left behind me,
And a new life I forsook.

For though the journey was long,

And at times I felt alone,
I knew that light was leading me,
To a place I could call home.

And now I stand before it,
That light that shone so bright,
And though the future's uncertain,
I know I'll be alright.

For I've learned that in the darkness,
When everything seems lost,
There's always a light ahead,
No matter what the cost.

I'll keep walking towards it,
With all my heart and soul,
And though the road is winding,
I'll let that light make me whole.

Hope in the Horizon

I walk the path that lies ahead
Though I know not where it leads
I leave behind what once was dead
And embrace the hope that feeds

The light in the horizon glows
A beacon of what's to come
It beckons me, and onward goes
Toward the future that's begun

The scars I bear, they weigh me down
The memories, they haunt my soul
But I won't let them wear a frown
I'll find my way to reach my goal

I'll face the trials, and rise above
The challenges that lay ahead
For I am strong, and filled with love
And hope will be my daily bread

With each step forward, I gain ground
The darkness fades, the light draws near
I know in my heart, I will be found
In a place where there is no fear

The road ahead may not be straight

But I will journey on, with faith
I'll overcome, and not abate
For the hope in my heart won't wraith

I see the sun rise in the east
The dawn of a brand new day
The light within me, it won't cease
For hope will guide me all the way

I'll leave behind the pain and strife
And embrace what's yet to be
For hope will be my guide in life
And lead me to a destiny

I'll keep walking, one step at a time
Toward the horizon where hope abounds
For I know that the light will shine
And a new world will be found.

Embracing the Unknown

As I stand here, alone and strong,
Gazing into the future, where I don't belong,
My heart is aching with sadness and pain,
For a love that was lost, that can't be regained.

But I know I'll face it, head held high,
For the unknown can't bring me down,
can't make me cry.
For just as my life thus far has taught,
Love is the power that can never be bought.

I'll take on the journey ahead,
Through every twist and turn, through every dread,
For like I have so rightly said,
I'll face what's to come, with grace and stead.

For my love was strong,
And I'll keep the flame burning, though you're gone.
For my love is the anchor that keeps me grounded,
Through every uncharted sea, every path unfounded.

I'll embrace the unknown, with courage and faith,
For I know there's a future beyond this dark wraith.
And face whatever comes, with open arms,
For my love will be my shield, against any harm.

I'll take on the future, with all its mystery,
With every challenge, every twist in my history,
For love, it is the power that sets me free,
In the unknown, I'll find my destiny.

Though our love may be over, and we've said our goodbyes,
I'll still look to the future, with hope in my eyes.
For love never truly dies, it just changes form,
And I'll keep it alive, through every storm.

I'll keep embracing the unknown, as I move forward,
With my heart open, my soul restored.
For love is the power that makes me strong,
And with it, I'll face the unknown, where I belong.

I Moved On, Now What?

I moved on, but the question remains,
What is the future, what's left to gain?
When a love is lost, what's left to see,
In the vast unknown that lies before me.

The pain is gone, but the memories remain,
Echoes of a love that will never be the same.
Yet I know, as I look ahead,
That the future is not yet written, not yet dead.

For the future is a canvas, yet to be painted,
A blank slate, yet to be tainted.
And though the past may hold its grip,
The future still offers a new script.

So I look to the future, with hope and faith,
For a new love, for a new place.
A place where I can finally belong,
A love that will be my guiding song.

For love, it is the power that makes us strong,
The light that guides us through the unknown.
And though the journey may be long,
Love will keep us steady, keep us strong.

I move on, with a heart open wide,

With a soul ready, with a new stride.

For the future is unknown, but it's not alone,

For love, it is the power that will lead us home.

I moved on, but I still carry the past,

For it's a part of who I am, it's a part of my path.

But the future, it's a new beginning,

A chance to find a new love, a chance to keep winning.

I move forward, with my head held high,

With a heart that's open, with a soul that's alive.

For the future, it's a new dawn,

And I'll keep moving on, until the old is gone.

Time For Healing & Writing

It's important to take time to process your emotions and find ways to heal. Writing can be a powerful tool for self-expression and reflection during this process. The guided open-ended prompts following this page, are designed to help you explore your feelings, gain clarity, and find closure.

Writing is a cathartic way to process your thoughts and feelings in a safe and private space. It allows you to explore your emotions without fear of judgment or interruption. Through writing, you can gain a deeper understanding of yourself and your situation. You may even discover insights and perspectives you didn't realize before. These prompts are meant to be fluid, allowing you to write freely and follow your thoughts wherever they may lead. There are no right or wrong answers, and you don't have to share your writing with anyone unless you choose to. By taking the time to reflect on these question-like prompts and write out your responses, you can release some of the pain and find a way forward. Remember to be gentle with yourself as you go through this process and take all the time you need to heal.

If you're just starting to process your emotions or looking for a way to work through lingering pain, the next series of writing prompts can serve as a writing or thought-provoking outlet to help you move forward and begin the healing process.

The hardest thing about the breakup has been...

When I think about my ex-partner, I still feel...

If I could say one thing to my ex-partner, it would be...

The thing I miss most about the relationship is...

The thing I am most afraid of now that the relationship is over is...

I am proud of myself for...

When I think about the future, I feel...

I wish I had known this before the breakup happened...

The thing I am looking forward to the most now that the relationship is over is...

The thing that brings me the most comfort during this time is...

I ADMIT TO THE FOLLOWING

I regret not communicating my needs more clearly.

I realized that I was the one who always made compromises.

I wish I had spent more time being present with you.

I ignored the red flags because I was afraid of being alone.

I should have listened to my intuition about us.

I never really felt like you truly understood me.

I took you for granted and now I see how much you meant to me.

I didn't know how to handle conflict in a healthy way.

I didn't prioritize our relationship and I regret it.

I became complacent and stopped putting in effort.

I allowed our differences to drive us apart.

I wasn't emotionally available for you when you needed me.

I realize now that we weren't compatible in the ways I hoped we would be.

I wish I had worked on my own issues before getting into a relationship.

I was too afraid to be vulnerable with you.

I see now that we both had different expectations for the relationship.

I struggled with jealousy and it affected our relationship.

I didn't respect your boundaries.

One thing that surprised me about the breakup was...

Over and over in my head, I keep replaying the moment when...

I feel like the only thing keeping me going is...

The thing that scares me the most about the future is...

I never realized how much I relied on my ex-partner for...

I wish I had told my ex-partner...

The most important thing I learned from the relationship is...

One thing I think would have made a difference in the relationship is...

The thing I am most grateful for right now is...

I am most worried about how the breakup will affect...

I wish I could go back in time and...

The thing that brings me the most joy right now is...

I feel like I lost a part of myself when...

The thing that has surprised me the most about myself since the breakup is...

I am most afraid of being alone because...

The thing that makes me most angry about the breakup is...

I feel like the breakup has changed me in the following ways...

Sometimes I feel like I am never going to be able to...

The thing that makes me the saddest about the breakup is...

CHECK ONE

☐ Love	or	☐ Hate
☐ Happy	or	☐ Sad
☐ Optimistic	or	☐ Pessimistic
☐ Trusting	or	☐ Suspicious
☐ Acceptance	or	☐ Denial
☐ Relief	or	☐ Regret
☐ Content	or	☐ Restless
☐ Confident	or	☐ Insecure
☐ Empowered	or	☐ Powerless
☐ Inspired	or	☐ Discouraged
☐ Free	or	☐ Trapped
☐ Independent	or	☐ Dependent
☐ Energized	or	☐ Drained
☐ Open	or	☐ Closed
☐ Forgiving	or	☐ Resentful
☐ Understanding	or	☐ Judgmental
☐ Peaceful	or	☐ Anxious
☐ Strong	or	☐ Fragile
☐ Grateful	or	☐ Unappreciative
☐ Excited	or	☐ Indifferent

I am most afraid of never being able to find someone who...

The thing that brings me the most comfort right now is...

I never realized how much I took...for granted until now.

The thing that scares me the most about the breakup is...

I feel like I could have done more to save the relationship by...

I am most worried about how my friends/family will react to the breakup because...

I never realized how much I relied on the relationship for...

Sometimes I wonder if my ex-partner ever...

The thing that makes me the happiest about the breakup is...

I wish I could forget about...

I am most afraid of being alone because...

I wish I had known sooner that...

The thing that has surprised me the most about my ex-partner since the breakup is...

I never realized how much I needed...until now.

The thing that has surprised me the most about myself since the breakup is...

I feel like I lost a part of myself when...

I am most afraid of never being able to trust someone again because...

The thing that makes me most angry about the breakup is...

Sometimes I feel like I am never going to be able to...

The thing that makes me the saddest about the breakup is...

I feel like the breakup has changed me in the following ways...

The thing that scares me the most about the future is...

I am most worried about how the breakup will impact my future plans for...

I never realized how much I sacrificed for the relationship until...

The thing that has surprised me the most about the breakup is...

I am most afraid of how the breakup will affect my self-esteem because...

The thing that has been the hardest to let go of is...

Sometimes I feel like the breakup was my fault because...

I wish I had known how to communicate my needs better by...

The thing that gives me hope for the future is...

I feel like I have lost my sense of...

The thing that makes me feel most vulnerable right now is...

I wish I had realized how important...was to me before the breakup.

I am most afraid of never finding someone who understands me the way my ex-partner did because...

The thing that has been the biggest challenge since the breakup is...

Sometimes I feel like my life is over because...

The thing that makes me feel most alone right now is...

I wish I had taken more time to focus on...

I never realized how much the relationship impacted my daily routine until...

The thing that has been the most unexpected consequence of the breakup is...

I feel like the breakup has forced me to confront...

The thing that has been the most difficult to process is...

Sometimes I wonder if the relationship was ever really...

I wish I had been more honest about my feelings by...

The thing that gives me the most strength during this time is...

I feel like the breakup has given me the opportunity to...

The thing that scares me the most about moving on is...

I never realized how much the relationship impacted my sense of identity until now.

The thing that has been the most comforting during this time is...

I wish I had listened to my instincts when...

I am most afraid of never being able to find happiness again because...

The thing that has been the most healing during this time is...

Sometimes I feel like the breakup was a blessing in disguise because...

The thing that has surprised me the most about myself since the breakup is...

I wish I had been more assertive about my needs by...

The thing that gives me the most hope for the future is...

I feel like the breakup has made me appreciate...

The thing that has been the most difficult to accept is...

Sometimes I wonder if my ex-partner ever truly understood...

I wish I had taken more time to focus on my own personal growth by...

The thing that scares me the most about the future is...

I never realized how much the relationship impacted my mental health until now.

The thing that has been the most surprising source of support during this time is...

I wish I had been more vulnerable with my ex-partner by...

The thing that gives me the most strength during this time is...

I feel like the breakup has given me the opportunity to focus on...

The thing that scares me the most about starting over is...

Sometimes I wonder if my ex-partner ever truly appreciated...

The thing that has been the most unexpected benefit of the breakup is...

I wish I had realized sooner that I am deserving of...

The thing I miss most about my ex-partner is...

I wish I had known how to express my love for my ex-partner by...

The thing that has been the most difficult to explain to others is...

Sometimes I feel like I am stuck in the past because...

I am most worried about how the breakup will affect our mutual friends because...

The thing that has been the most difficult to forgive myself for is...

I wish I had spent more time getting to know myself before the relationship by...

The thing that has been the most difficult to accept is that...

Sometimes I feel like my ex-partner was the only one who really understood...

I am most afraid of never being able to trust someone again because...

The thing that has been the most surprising thing I've learned about myself since the breakup is...

I wish I had been more patient with my ex-partner by...

The thing that has been the most difficult to let go of is...

Sometimes I feel like I will never be able to move on because...

I am most worried about how the breakup will affect my family because...

The thing that has been the most difficult to talk about with my ex-partner is...

I wish I had known how to communicate better with my ex-partner by...

The thing that has been the most surprising thing I've learned about my ex-partner since the breakup is...

Sometimes I feel like my ex-partner was the only one who really knew how to...

I am most afraid of being alone forever because...

The thing that has been the most difficult to accept about my ex-partner is...

I wish I had been more forgiving with my ex-partner by...

The thing that has been the most unexpected source of support during this time is...

Sometimes I feel like the breakup was a wake-up call for me to...

I am most worried about how the breakup will affect my career because...

The thing that has been the most difficult to come to terms with is...

I wish I had taken more time to nurture my friendships during the relationship by...

The thing that has been the most healing for me during this time is...

Sometimes I feel like my ex-partner was the only one who really cared about...

I am most afraid of never being able to feel happy again because...

The thing that has been the most difficult to explain to myself is...

I wish I had been more supportive of my ex-partner's dreams by...

The thing that has been the most unexpected thing to come out of the breakup is...

Sometimes I feel like the breakup has changed me in ways I don't fully understand because...

I am most worried about how the breakup will affect my financial situation because...

The thing that has been the most difficult to express to my ex-partner is...

I wish I had known how to compromise better during the relationship by...

The thing that has been the most surprising thing I've learned about relationships since the breakup is...

Sometimes I feel like the breakup was a reflection of my own shortcomings because...

I am most afraid of losing touch with who I am because...

The thing that has been the most difficult to understand about my ex-partner's perspective is...

I wish I had known how to show my appreciation for my ex-partner by...

The thing that has been the most surprising thing I've learned about myself since the breakup is...

Sometimes I feel like my ex-partner was the only...

I am most worried about how the breakup will affect my future plans because...

The thing that has been the most difficult to process is...

I wish I had been more open-minded during the relationship by...

The thing that has been the most unexpected challenge since the breakup is...

Sometimes I feel like the breakup was inevitable because...

I am most afraid of repeating the same mistakes in my next relationship because...

ON A SCALE OF ONE to TEN

Heartbroken	1	2	3	4	5	6	7	8	9	10
Betrayed	1	2	3	4	5	6	7	8	9	10
Lonely	1	2	3	4	5	6	7	8	9	10
Confused	1	2	3	4	5	6	7	8	9	10
Devastated	1	2	3	4	5	6	7	8	9	10
Angry	1	2	3	4	5	6	7	8	9	10
Lost	1	2	3	4	5	6	7	8	9	10
Rejected	1	2	3	4	5	6	7	8	9	10
Insecure	1	2	3	4	5	6	7	8	9	10
Vulnerable	1	2	3	4	5	6	7	8	9	10
At Peace	1	2	3	4	5	6	7	8	9	10
Relieved	1	2	3	4	5	6	7	8	9	10
Hopeful	1	2	3	4	5	6	7	8	9	10
Excited	1	2	3	4	5	6	7	8	9	10
Healed	1	2	3	4	5	6	7	8	9	10

Made in the USA
Coppell, TX
17 April 2023

15732755R00100